Original title:
Carve It Like It's Snow Tomorrow

Copyright © 2024 Creative Arts Management OÜ
All rights reserved.

Author: Maxwell Donovan
ISBN HARDBACK: 978-9916-94-186-7
ISBN PAPERBACK: 978-9916-94-187-4

Transforming Silence into Crystal Design

In a world where quiet reigns,
Laughter bubbles like champagne.
Chipping away at frosty forms,
Silly shapes in winter's charms.

Snowflakes giggle, dance around,
Whispering secrets, soft and sound.
With each push, a joyful cheer,
Turned to ice, our dreams appear.

The Sculptor's Heart in the Winter Gale

The wind howls like a playful pup,
Snowballs form, let's give them a hup!
A block of ice, a vision quite wild,
A penguin statue, a winter child.

Chisels clash in merry delight,
Sculptor grins, it feels just right.
With each crack, we laugh and shout,
Who knew cold could bring such clout?

Frost-etched Wishes: Crafting Tomorrow's Glow

Underneath the frost-stained moon,
We giggle like we'll leave too soon.
Crafting wishes by candlelight,
A snowman dances, what a sight!

With a carrot nose and goofy grin,
Making snow angels, let the fun begin.
Each frosty breath, we carve with glee,
A winter dream, wild and free.

Enchanted by Winter's Tender Touch

Winter whispers with a fluffy sigh,
Tickling cheeks as snowflakes fly.
With a snow shovel, we start our play,
Creating chaos in a blissful way.

A snow fort army, ready for war,
Snowball fights, who could ask for more?
Laughter erupts like a gentle storm,
Sheltering joy in every form.

Anticipating Tomorrow's White Embrace

Piling on layers, I grace the chill,
Hoping tomorrow, I'll slide down a hill.
Snowflakes keep whispering, soft and bright,
But I'm a snowman waiting for flight.

Dreams of snowball fights make me chuckle,
With my carrot nose, I'll dodge that buckle.
Laughter will echo as we tumble and play,
All while the flakes twirl and dance in ballet.

Scattered Snow, Gathered Dreams

Clouds are gossiping, with secrets to share,
A sprinkle of white, like frosting in the air.
Snowflakes giggle, as they dance and swoon,
While I wonder if it'll all melt by noon.

On this frigid canvas, I sketch up a plan,
To catch every flake, oh, the joy of the span!
But once I reach out, they vanish like steam,
My snowball ambitions burst, what a scheme!

A Future Wrapped in Frosted Layers

Tomorrow may bring a thrilling delight,
Flurries may blanket me through the night.
With mittens and hats, I'm geared for the test,
But let's hope my nose won't surrender to frost's jest.

Waking at dawn, I peek through the pane,
The world bathed in white, it looks like a gain!
Yet, leap from the bed, what do I see?
A mountain of laundry, oh, where's my spree?

Etching Our Stories in Winter's Silence

Quiet the world, as snow covers the ground,
With snowy tales waiting to be found.
We'll draw in the drifts, our laughter will soar,
Creating a masterpiece, right at our door.

But wait! What's that? A snowplow's roar!
Your masterpiece is gone, swept out from the floor.
Yet with every flake, new stories will rise,
In this frosty playground, giggles are our prize.

Serenity in the Snowbound Silence

Frosty blankets cover the ground,
Children giggle, laughter all around.
Snowmen wobble, hats askew,
A carrot nose that once was blue.

Sleds zoom past in a wild race,
With snowballs hurled at lightning pace.
A slip, a fall, a frosty swirl,
Winter magic gives a twirl!

Frozen Frames of Future Bliss

Snap a pic in the chilly air,
Duck face poses, snow in my hair.
A frozen smile, tongue out wide,
Caught mid-flop from an epic slide.

Hot cocoa spills, marshmallows fly,
A snowball fight, oh me, oh my!
Laughter rings, we'll face the cold,
These frosty tales will never grow old.

Shaping the Icy Dawn Ahead

Morning light, the snow starts to gleam,
Snowflakes dancing, a winter dream.
Plowing paths with a goofy grin,
Catching snowflakes upon my chin.

Pine trees wear their frosty gowns,
Squirrels scamper, oh how they frown.
But with a wink and a snowball's toss,
Winter fun is never a loss!

Whispers of Winter's Promise

Underneath the powdery white,
Lies the promise of pure delight.
Giggling friends, we throw and squeal,
In this winter wonder, we spin and reel.

Hot cheeks, red noses, oh what a sight!
A snowman looks on, feeling quite bright.
As twilight falls, we gather near,
With winter whispers, we'll share a cheer!

Whirlwind of Winter's Imprint

A snowman with a top hat sway,
He's dancing in the breeze today.
With buttons made of coal and glee,
He's stealing all the joy for free.

The snowball fight is on, oh dear,
Laughter ringing loud and clear.
The flakes are flying, wild and bright,
Who knew winter could be such a delight?

Frost-Bound Fantasies

The squirrel in a winter coat,
Struts about with grand new hope.
He's hiding nuts in snowy drifts,
Counting on those winter gifts.

The ice rink cracks, a playful shout,
Did someone bring the penguins out?
They whirl and twirl, with joy abound,
While we slip and slide upon the ground.

Designing a Snowflake's Journey

Each snowflake has a tale to spin,
Drifting down, it twirls with a grin.
It lands on noses, hats, and trees,
Making winter a grand tease.

The flurries twinkle, dance, and play,
Turning the world a frosty gray.
Not a single one will go unturned,
For laughter is the fire we've burned.

Molding Tomorrow Beneath Winter's Veil

In the cold, we shape our dreams,
Into goofy shapes, or so it seems.
The snowman's got a carrot nose,
But whispers secrets that nobody knows.

The festive cheer spills through the night,
With mugs of cocoa, what a sight!
Laughter echoes, a frosty cheer,
As winter's veil brings us all near.

Tracing Echoes in a Frozen Realm

In a land where snowflakes waddle,
Footprints like penguins play and dawdle.
Laughter rises, cold air sparkles,
We slip and slide, like silly marbles.

Snowmen wearing funny hats and ties,
With carrot noses, oh my, oh my!
Sledding down hills, we scream in glee,
Bumps and jumps, like life's a spree.

Snowballs flying, dodging here and there,
A fluffy barrage, without a care.
With cheeks aglow and toes quite numb,
We giggle and dance, winter's just begun!

Crystalline Journeys of the Heart

On journeys through the frosty haze,
We twirl and spin in the sun's warm rays.
Ice skates glide, a comical dance,
Falling in heaps, but taking a chance.

Hot cocoa spills, marshmallows fly,
Laughter erupts, it's do or die!
Melting hearts like chocolate bars,
Soaring high on winter's stars.

Chasing snowflakes, each a thrill,
Why not catch one? Just for the skill!
With giggles echoing all around,
In frozen dreams, our joy is found.

Snowflakes Fall, Futures Form

Tiny crystals, fluttering down,
Dressing the world, nature's own crown.
Every flake is a story to share,
Silly shapes cause us to stare.

We build forts of laughter, and snow,
With cotton white fluff, we put on a show.
Throwing snowballs like friendly shots,
With every splat, we forget our thoughts.

In a snow globe, we spin and glide,
Caught in a whirlwind, it's quite a ride!
And as we tumble, joyously fall,
We find our futures, through it all.

Formed by Frost's Gentle Hand

Frosty patterns dance on glass,
Kids knock on doors, let's have a blast!
With playful giggles, we build and mold,
A kingdom of laughter in the cold.

Snowflakes whisper, "Catch me now!"
As we chase them, we laugh and bow.
Frosty moustaches and hats aflight,
Let's have a snowball fight tonight!

With each stumble, we wobble and sway,
Creating moments that brighten our day.
So grab your mittens, let the fun start,
In the chill of winter, we warm our hearts!

Crafting Tomorrow in Icy Hues

With spoons and forks we start to play,
Creating shapes in icy spray.
A snowman winks, he's got a hat,
He steals a carrot from the cat.

We giggle as we build the throne,
A frosty palace made of bone.
Sleds become our royal steeds,
Racing down the hill like weeds.

The chilly air makes noses red,
While laughter bounces in our heads.
Snowflakes dance like tiny stars,
As we paint winter into ours.

So grab your tools, don't be shy,
Let's sculpt the clouds as they float by.
In hues of blue and shades of white,
We'll make tomorrow feel just right.

The Brush of Winter's Whisper

A paintbrush made from frosty air,
Brush strokes float without a care.
Whispers swirl where laughter's found,
In winter's grip, we twirl around.

Snowflakes giggle when they fall,
Creating music, a frozen call.
With every splash a story grows,
Of gingerbread and hot cocoa woes.

Pine trees added with a wink,
Dancing rainbows on the brink.
We sprinkle glitter, just for fun,
As chilly breezes spin and run.

Let's splash the world in shimmering snow,
Like artists wild, we let it flow.
With every snowy brush of fate,
We laugh, we play, and celebrate.

Chilled Horizons: A Frozen Canvas

Look out! A sled is on the run,
With giggles echoing just for fun.
Our canvas stretches wide and free,
Snowmen posing like royalty.

With a flip, we build a mound,
Tender frosty hugs abound.
Our spirits rise like flurries do,
In winter's arms, we spin anew.

Penguins sliding, what a sight,
Making memories, pure delight.
With every throw of fluffy snow,
Winter's art begins to glow.

So gather round, let's take a chance,
In this frosty, silly dance.
With chilly strokes, we shall create,
A masterpiece to celebrate.

Melodies of Flurries and Shadows

Hark! The winter's music plays,
In melodies of chilly days.
Snowflakes tap upon our doors,
Like little elves on winter's shores.

Chasing shadows, we take flight,
With laughter filling up the night.
A snowball fight, but who will win?
With every hit, we freeze and grin.

While twinkling stars peek from above,
We find our joy in this silly love.
With puffy coats and frozen toes,
Let's make winter our merry prose.

So share your dreams in icy verse,
Let's paint the world with joy, not worse.
In this snowy wonderland we roam,
Together, we'll always find our home.

The Artistry of Winter's Breath

With mittens on and cheeks aglow,
The snowflakes dance, a chilly show.
I tried to catch one in my palm,
But slipped on ice, it all went wrong.

My snowman looks like a lumpy hat,
A carrot nose with a cheeky spat.
His eyes of coal, a crooked grin,
It seems he's laughing at my spin.

Snowballs fly with joyous glee,
I duck and weave, but who's to see?
A snowball strikes my unsuspecting friend,
Now I'm the target; this won't end!

The winter sky, a pastel dream,
But I'm knee-deep in frosty cream.
We laugh and roll, in nature's play,
Till winter whispers, "End of day."

Echoes of a Snowy Silence

The world is white, a quiet cheer,
But wait, what's that? A flick of fear!
A squirrel darts with nuts to hide,
In this stillness, laughter does abide.

I build a fort, my icy shield,
But who'd have guessed? I'm soon revealed.
A snowball fight breaks out in spree,
While I just wanted peace and glee!

The crunch of snow, a symphony,
Each step I take is pure comedy.
I slide, I fall, I clumsily roll,
Nature's jest takes a heavy toll.

But laughter rings through the chilly air,
Snowflakes twirl, without a care.
The quiet echoes, full of cheer,
'Cause winter can be goofy, dear!

Shaping Dreams in a Crystal Breeze

In my dreams, I mold the snow,
A castle fit for a royal show.
But reality bites, my shovel's stuck,
This fluffy pile just brings bad luck.

Snowmen wobble, their hats askew,
With a sock for a scarf—oh that's just cruel!
The kids are giggling, making a mess,
As I chase them round, my frozen dress!

We skate on ponds that tease and mock,
One step forward, then it's shock!
I twirl and glide, but soon I'll fall,
Winter comedy, the best of all.

So let us laugh through flakes galore,
Winter's charm opened every door.
With friends around, the cold is bright,
In a frosty world, we'll find our light.

In the Heart of the Frosted Silence

The evening hush, a snowy glow,
I set out to build a friend from snow.
But wait! A plop, a drip, a sound,
My frosty creation hits the ground!

With every scoop, my hopes take flight,
But now my snowman is a snow fright.
His head rolled off, a bouncy ball,
And now he's playing, "Catch" with all!

The snowflakes fall, a frosted choir,
I wear a grin, full of desire.
With laughter ringing in the air,
The winter chill can't hide our flair.

So let's embrace this winter day,
With slickened boots, and childlike play.
Through snowy smiles, we dance anew,
In the heart of frost, where dreams come true!

The Silent Symphony of Chilled Silence

In the quiet of the night,
Snowflakes dance in pale moonlight.
With giggles echoing all around,
The whispers in the frosty ground.

Snowmen totter, hats askew,
Carrots laughing at their view.
As snowball fights break out in frolic,
The chill turns into something comic.

Sleds tumble, kids in a heap,
With giggles sent into a sweep.
Frosty breath in chilly air,
Such joy spills with every dare.

Winter's song, a merry tune,
Laughter sparkles like the moon.
With every snowdrift, whims arise,
In this frosty wonder, we capsize.

Celestial Patterns in the Frost

Stars above in snowy skies,
Twinkling like our crazy tries.
Angels made of frosty fluff,
We're convinced we're cool enough.

Snowflakes land, a fuzzy kiss,
In this winter's chilly bliss.
Hot cocoa sips, a silly grin,
Who knew cold could hold such win?

Winter coats that fit just right,
Dancing like it's pure delight.
Mittens lost in the great white sea,
Every tumble brings out glee.

Snowy art, a canvas bright,
With every throw, we spark a fight.
Laughter echoes, joy through frost,
In our chilly world, we're never lost.

Crafting Dreams in Icy Stillness

In the icy grip of night,
Dreams are crafted, pure delight.
With frozen mugs of laughter wide,
We slide down hills on winter's tide.

Snowflakes stick like silly glue,
Twirling like they have no clue.
Frosty mustaches, dashing flair,
In the cold, we're debonair.

Snow forts rise, a great defense,
Against surprise and crazy suspense.
As kids collide in muffled cheer,
The winter's magic draws us near.

Midnight snacks of crunchy snow,
With giggles echoing, off we go.
Each icy breath, a silly chime,
We freeze in moments, capture time.

Frosted Dreams in a World Awakened

Awake to morning wrapped in white,
The world's a canvas, pure delight.
With slippers sliding on the floor,
The fresh chill makes us want much more.

Laughter echoes through the frost,
In frozen jeans, we're never lost.
Snowflakes fall, a pillow fight,
Wrapped in fun till late at night.

Hot treats bubbling, warming us,
As wintery winds create a fuss.
Sleds are racing, laughter swells,
With icy cheekbones, magic dwells.

Frosty windows, patterns drawn,
As gleeful hearts greet every dawn.
In this frosted dream, we play,
In a world awakened, come what may.

Frost-Kissed Memories: A Sculptor's Tale

With a shovel and a grin, I plunge,
The snowflakes giggle, they swirl and sponge.
A snowman's hat that's way too tall,
I'm quite the artist, or so I call.

My carrot nose is slightly bent,
The neighbors laugh, it's all well-meant.
With arms of sticks, they wiggle, sway,
Oh look, it's dancing—hip-hip-hooray!

But as the sun begins to peek,
My frosty friend starts to feel weak.
A puddle laughs, a watery face,
'This was fun, but now I'm displaced.'

So next year, I'll try yet again,
With a better hat and lots more grain.
For snowmen dreams will always gleam,
In the winter, we share the same team.

Beneath the Snow: Echoes of Tomorrow

Under a blanket of fluffy white,
A surprise awaits, it's pure delight.
Snowball battles break out like wars,
I'll build a fortress with icy doors.

With boots of rubber and mittens bright,
We transform the yard, oh what a sight!
The give-and-take of a snowball flight,
Giggles erupt in the chilly night.

Then comes the moment of gliding fast,
On sleds we sail, a joy unsurpassed.
Yet, one grand trip sends me off track,
Into a snowdrift—oh, what a whack!

At day's end, when all's said and done,
The frost bites clear, but we've had our fun.
Forever echoes, our laughter stay,
Memories made, come out to play.

Serenity in Sculpted Snow

In dusk's calm light, I start to shape,
A peaceful form, like nature's grape.
Frosty fingers reach out, so kind,
A frozen friend, not one of humankind.

With a swirl here and a twist on the side,
My snow companion glows with pride.
But soon he's sliding, making a fuss,
I swear he's got a mind—so much to discuss!

Lay down and see the snowflakes dance,
A whirlwind wonder, a snowy romance.
With every flake, a giggle drops,
Oh! What a game, till my talent stops.

The night creeps in, and sculptures loom,
While I sit back and admire the gloom.
In snow-capped beauty, laughter still rings,
Peace reigns when winter sweetly sings.

The Lullaby of Frosted Edges

Whispering winds of a frosty night,
Lullabies come with soft, snowy light.
Gloves on a mission, a world to build,
With snow in pockets, my heart is filled.

Icicles hanging like chandeliers,
Cackling like crows, we're all wild peers.
Creating castles, erecting dreams,
With frosty fingers, nothing's as it seems.

But hours pass, and the sun will rise,
Turning my empire to soft, gooey pies.
'Twas fun while it lasted', I cheer and shout,
'Next winter, I'll build—without a doubt!'

So here's a toast to the winter scene,
Where laughter and snow make the world pristine.
Let's wait for tomorrow, it'll come anew,
For winter's magic will see us through.

Chisel the Icy Echoes

When frosty winds begin to blow,
We grab our tools, our spirits glow.
With laughter loud, we start to play,
As icy sculptures steal the day.

A penguin here, a snowman there,
The faces we shape, with silly flair.
Each flake a giggle, each drift a cheer,
In frozen fun, we shed a tear.

With chisels high and spirits bright,
We dance around in pure delight.
A frosty slip, a snowball fight,
Our winter wonderland ignites.

So come together, shout and scream,
In this crisp world, we'll chase a dream.
With snowy smiles and frosty cheer,
We carve our joy, year after year.

Sculpting Dreams in Winter's Grasp

In winter's grip, when all is white,
We gather round 'neath pale moonlight.
With shovels high and hearts so bold,
We shape our dreams in glints of cold.

A dragon here, a unicorn's horn,
In snowy realms, our hopes are born.
With laughter mixed into the snow,
The wacky shapes begin to grow.

Our sculpting skills, a curious sight,
As snowballs soar and snowmen fight.
With every piece, a joke in place,
We'll laugh until we lose our grace.

So bring your whimsy, bring your flair,
In every flake, there's joy to share.
With frozen fingers and grins so wide,
We'll dance in snow, our dreams our guide.

Etching Hope on the Frozen Canvas

On this canvas, crisp and clean,
We etch our hopes, a funny scene.
With icy breath and playful minds,
In every glob, a smile finds.

A beard of snow, a hat askew,
With jagged edges, laughter grew.
Our frosty art, a sight to see,
With every curve, a memory.

Oh, tip-tap toes on icy ground,
We slip and spin, twirl around.
A frosty face mid giggle burst,
In winter's revelry, we trust.

So seize the moment, don't be shy,
Let every chuckle lift you high.
In snowflakes dancing, joy shall bloom,
Let's fill our hearts, dispel the gloom.

Tomorrow's Chill, Today's Artistry

As tomorrow's frost begins to creep,
We set to work, while others sleep.
With icy fingers, we create,
A masterpiece, we can't be late!

The sculptures rise, with comical flair,
A snow giraffe with nappy hair.
With frosty noses and silly hats,
Our icy crew, all cuddly cats.

With every slip, we burst in glee,
For in this chill, we feel so free.
Tomorrow's freeze won't dull our art,
We'll laugh and play and share our heart.

So gather round, let's make a scene,
In winter's night, where life's a dream.
Our whimsical world, a joyful quest,
In sculpting fun, we feel so blessed.

Sculpting Hopes in the Snowfall Light

With shovels raised like wands of cheer,
We sculpt our dreams, oh so sincere.
Snowflakes fall, a giggling crew,
Making snowmen, one, two, and woo!

Frosty noses, they wink and smile,
As we slip and slide, oh what a style!
Armfuls of snow become glorious sights,
Who knew winter could bring such delights?

Chubby cheeks, rosy and bright,
Rolling in snow, what a silly sight!
We create a kingdom, frosty and grand,
In a world where snowballs rule the land!

As dusk approaches, we laugh and play,
Now the snowmen keep watch till the day.
In our icy haven, we reign supreme,
Who knew winter could fulfill a dream?

The Dreamer's Canvas in Frost

On winter's canvas, pure and wide,
We splash around with giggly pride.
Hats askew and scarves in a knot,
A masterpiece? Not a chance, I thought!

Snowflakes swirl like playful friends,
We shape on whims, where laughter bends.
With carrot noses and eyes of coal,
Our frosty figures take on a role!

Sleds careen down icy hills,
Chasing thrills with twirls and spills.
Each tumble brings a gleeful shout,
Who knew white stuff could bring such clout?

As night falls softly, stars do gleam,
In this wintry art, we find our theme.
Every snowman stands tall and proud,
In our frosty gallery, we laugh out loud!

Mapping Tomorrow in White Trails

We trace our plans in snow so light,
Carefree paths in the frosty night.
With every step, a giggle breaks,
As snowflakes fall, our joy awakes.

The hills are calling, so off we fly,
Sliding down like a cheerful sigh.
Wipe the snow from a cheeky grin,
Every fall just makes us spin!

Snow angels flutter, wings spread wide,
In a world where silliness won't hide.
With snowballs flying, we dodge and weave,
Who knew winter could be so naive?

Tomorrow's dreams mapped out in frost,
With laughter shared, we are never lost.
Each winter venture brings endless cheer,
In our snowy kingdom, let's persevere!

Iced Realities of Winter's Craft

With ice sickles hanging from the eaves,
We plot our pranks like winter thieves.
A stealthy walk on a frosty sheet,
Oops! Slipped and landed on my seat!

We gather, planning our best blend,
Who can toss snow with art to mend?
Snowball fights erupt with glee,
Watch out! You're now a snow-stuffed bee!

Each frosty breath a little cloud,
We paint the scene, laughter loud.
Winter's craft, both clumsy and sly,
A frosty show beneath the sky.

At day's end, our dreams align,
With snowflakes dancing, oh so fine.
In these icy moments, joy does last,
With goofy smiles, we have a blast!

Threads of Ice in the Tapestry of Time

In winter's grip, we dance and slide,
With frozen threads, we take our ride.
A patchwork quilt of frosty glee,
Stitching laughter, just you and me.

Snowflakes giggle as they fall,
A nature's prank, we heed the call.
We chase the flurries with a grin,
Creating chaos, let the fun begin!

Icicles hang like chandeliers,
Reflecting joy amidst our cheers.
We build our castles, all askew,
The rulers of ice, just me and you.

So let's embrace this chilly spree,
With whimsy woven, wild and free.
For time's a canvas, winter's gift,
In every slip, our spirits lift.

In the Wake of Snowy Dreams

As snowflakes dance, we twirl around,
With fluffy dreams upon the ground.
We slip and slide, a frosty show,
In our pajamas, oh what a glow!

The dog dives in, a snowy splash,
While we all giggle at the crash.
A snowball fight, we take our aim,
Who knew winter could be a game?

The snowman's arms are twigs and glee,
He's waving goodbyes with stylish flair.
A carrot nose, a tilted grin,
In snowy scenes, we all fit in.

So let's embrace this winter whim,
Where every day feels like a hymn.
In snowy dreams, we'll find our way,
Creating smiles on every play.

The Design of Tomorrow's Frost

A blanket of white, the world's a stage,
With frosty outlines, we engage.
A sketch of fun, in every drift,
Let's bundle up, we'll share the gift.

Hot cocoa steam and laughter roars,
As we race through open doors.
The art of snowflakes, shapes galore,
Their icy beauty we all adore.

Sleds zoom by, a merry chase,
With rosy cheeks, we find our place.
A frozen canvas, we paint with cheer,
In the chilly air, our joy is clear.

With booted steps, we'll dance anew,
In every flake, there's fun for two.
So let's sketch memories, bold and bright,
In the white of day and the stars of night.

Tender Hues Beneath Winter's Whisper

Beneath the hush, a secret blooms,
In drifts of white, we find our rooms.
Laughter echoes, a crisp delight,
As we waddle around, what a sight!

Frosted branches, a quirky nod,
To winter's charms, we're all applauded.
We twinkle toes on icy trails,
With every slip, each giggle sails.

A snowman's grin, a jolly face,
Eager smiles in every place.
We craft our joy with gentle hands,
In the frosty breeze, our spirit stands.

So let us bask in winter's glow,
Where silliness is the star of show.
In tender hues, we find our song,
Embracing winter, where we belong.

Etched in Ice

A penguin in a bowtie,
Trying hard to dance,
Twisting all around,
In a frozen trance.

Snowflakes start to giggle,
As they land on his nose,
He slips and gives a chuckle,
As his partner froze.

Snowmen in a huddle,
Gossiping with glee,
Who'll be the next to tumble,
On this ice so free?

But when the sun comes out,
The dance must come to end,
Off to melt into puddles,
Just ask the snowman friend.

Bound by Time

Tick tock on the icicles,
Chilling tales now told,
Frosty clocks keep laughing,
At the young and old.

Mittens on a snowman,
Waving as they freeze,
They're always in a hurry,
To catch the winter breeze.

Got my scarf on backward,
Oh, the style I wear!
Laughter fills the frosty air,
As my friends just stare.

Time to warm the cocoa,
While cozy in the chair,
Just don't forget the marshmallows,
Or you might declare!

The Fragile Heart of Winter's Day

Ice cream cones for penguins,
On a chilly night,
They giggle, and they wobble,
In a frosty fright.

Snowflakes play a trumpet,
As they flit and sway,
Winter wear's a funny hat,
Oh, what a display!

But watch out for the puddles,
They'll take you for a ride,
Splashing like a dolphin,
With winter as your guide.

We'll toast marshmallows bright,
As they melt and sing,
In the fragile heart of winter,
We laugh at everything!

Future Shapes in the Glacial Night

Sculptures made of laughter,
In this icy land,
Dancing with the shadows,
In a winter band.

Oval-shaped like jellybeans,
Look! A slide appears,
The giggles echo loudly,
Breaking all the fears.

Snowflakes fall like feathers,
Tickling noses near,
As the shivers wander,
We all yell, "Oh dear!"

Through the glacial wonder,
Shapes just won't hold tight,
Tomorrow we'll be molding,
In our dream delight!

Snow-Covered Visions Waiting to Emerge

Huddled in the snowdrifts,
Gummy worms disguise,
They wait for spring's arrival,
With their tiny eyes.

Tobogganing squirrels giggle,
As they race by fast,
On their mini sleds made clear,
It's a snowy blast!

Caught within a snowball,
They plan their sly attack,
But the bird, so clever, laughs,
And dodges with a quack.

Snow-covered dreams are waiting,
They'll burst out in due time,
For now, let's just be silly,
And play in endless rhyme.

Tapestry of Tomorrow's Snowfall

Flakes drift down, a comic show,
They stick and slide, just like a pro.
Snowballs fly with cheeky grins,
While mittens get lost in snowy bins.

A snowman stands with a goofy face,
His carrot nose, now out of place.
Kids build castles, forts up high,
As snowflakes dance and tumble by.

Creating Myths in the Crystal White

In winter's glow, legends arise,
Of penguins with plans, and crafty spies.
Sledding down hills with giggles galore,
While hot cocoa waits, a sweet encore.

The snowflakes tell tales, they'd surely boast,
Of snowmen missing their scarves the most.
Yet laughter binds all that's absurd,
In this frosty realm, joy is preferred.

Beneath the Ice

Beneath the ice, where secrets hide,
Puns and giggles take a wild ride.
Skating around like a slippery fool,
While penguins offer to lend their rule.

The frozen lake sings a jolly tune,
As fish wiggle by, laughing with the moon.
What's that sound? A snowplow's roar,
Oops! There goes our snowball score!

Seeds of Tomorrow

Seeds of laughter scatter in snow,
Frosty jests, like stars, they glow.
Snowflakes tumble with a silly twist,
Who knew snow could be such a jest?

Twirl like a flake, embrace the cold,
In this realm, joy never gets old.
Giggles echo, as snowmen sway,
While winter laughs at yesterday.

Shaping Winter's Subtle Secrets

Winter whispers its quirky lore,
Of snowball fights and a snowman's snore.
Each flake a jest, each drift a delight,
Painting the world with snowy white.

In the charming chill, odd tales unfold,
About friendly yetis, both raucous and bold.
As laughter echoes on the snowy street,
Winter knows how to keep things sweet!

Frosty Reflections of a Season's Promise

In a world of frosty mirrors, we laugh,
As snowflakes dance like they're on a path.
Everyone slips in a graceful twirl,
Belly flops lead to a winter swirl.

Hot cocoa spills, but we're all aglow,
Sipping gingerly—didn't think it would flow!
Snowmen wearing hats, a bit askew,
With carrots wonky, oh what a view!

Sleds race by, oh what a sight,
A toasty bonfire warms us at night.
With marshmallows flying, what a joy,
We become giggling kids, oh boy!

Frosty reflections, we can't resist,
Making snow angels, how could we miss?
With laughter echoing through the cold,
Every chilly moment's a tale to be told.

Silhouettes in Winter's Light

Winter nights bring us funny shades,
Footprints in snow, where the laughter cascades.
Dancing shadows with mitten-clad friends,
Hide-and-seek chilly fun never ends.

Snowballs fly; dodge if you're wise,
Laughter erupts—oh, the snowy surprise!
Who knew a frostbite would bring such glee?
Between flurries, that snowball's for me!

Snowmen grinning, their noses a mess,
As we try to fashion the fluff in excess.
With a cheeky wink, and a crooked grin,
Winter's a stage where the fun will begin!

In silhouettes bold, we prance 'round the park,
Creating memories when it's icy and dark.
Funny moments etched in the white,
Mirth in the winter, pure delight!

The Icy Mosaics of Next Dawn

Morning light filters through frosty panes,
I see the chaos; it's hard to refrain.
Last night's snowball fight left us unshorn,
A mosaic of laughter, brightly worn.

Icicles dangle, like unicorn horns,
Dripping sparkles under the grey morns.
With every step, we crunch and glide,
Inventing a dance that we can't hide.

Snowflakes tickle, they cling to our nose,
In winter's embrace, we strike a pose.
Witty banter wrapped in woolly attire,
A flurry of giggles, we never tire.

The dawn reveals, our laughter in bloom,
Painting the world with snow's perfect plume.
As we tumble and roll, just being free,
In icy mosaics, it's joy that we see.

Communing with Tomorrow in the Snow

Each flake whispers secrets, we share a laugh,
In a wintery world, we're a quirky half.
Toboggans racing on slopes, oh yes!
Who will crash first? It's all just finesse!

Frosty adventures, adventures await,
We tumble and play; it's never too late.
Gather the crew, let's make a mistake,
With snowballs in hand, it's all for fun's sake.

Chunky mittens squeezing hot soup,
A belly full of joy—come join the troop!
With frozen giggles, we create our tale,
In the snow, we're all bound to prevail.

With each frosty morning, we see prior deeds,
As tomorrow awaits, fulfilling our needs.
Communing in laughter as the winter winds blow,
In this snowy paradise, our spirits all glow.

Frosted Shadows in the Twilight

In chilly dance, we laugh and play,
The snowman grins, come what may.
He lost his nose to a hungry crow,
A carrot snack, now here we go!

Snowball fights ignite the night,
Laughter echoes, pure delight.
But slippery paths, oh what a jest,
I'm sliding down, a frosty guest.

The dog acts like he's in a race,
With snowflakes hanging on his face.
He leaps and bounds, in joy, he roams,
Creating art with all our bones!

As twilight fades, we start to tire,
With frosted breath and hearts on fire.
Under starlit skies, the fun won't cease,
Let's make a snow angel, a frosty piece!

Chisel the Chill: A Winter's Embrace

With hats too big and scarves so bright,
We waddle around in pure delight.
A snowman contest, who can excel?
He's got a nose that's quite a tale to tell!

Hot cocoa spills, oh what a mess,
Marshmallows in our hair, I guess.
We build a fort, a cozy nook,
Not much defense, take another look!

Sledding down a hill too steep,
I wonder if I should just leap?
With belly flops, we gain some speed,
Oops! Went too far, did we mislead?

Nighttime falls, and we collapse,
Snowflakes falling, gentle laps.
In laughter's echo, winter's bliss,
A snowy hug, oh what a kiss!

Frosting the Canvas of Time

With tiny snowflakes racing down,
We bundle up in cozy gowns.
Each flake that lands, a point to score,
A winter game we can't ignore!

The trees wear coats, all white and neat,
But where's my glove? I can't find my feet!
A snowball flies, I duck too late,
But laughter follows—it's fate!

The mailman slips, oh what a sight,
While dogs bark joyfully at night.
With each crazy tumble and fall,
We rise again, oh we stand tall!

In frosted wonder, we lay it down,
Kid-like joy refuses to drown.
Let's paint the world with snowy grace,
In this winter wonderland, we embrace!

When the World Wears a Shroud of White

When morning breaks with white delight,
I throw on boots, it's Snow Day right!
The sun peeks through, we shout hooray,
In our winter wonderland, so gay!

The neighbors' cat, with grace distills,
Plays in the snow, ignoring spills.
She leaps and bounds, like she's in flight,
Every jump, a laugh, pure delight!

The icicles drip like frozen spears,
While sleds and laughter chase down fears.
The world transformed, our hearts alive,
In frosty fun, we truly thrive!

As shadows stretch and day turns night,
We dance and twirl in pure delight.
With snowflakes swirling through the air,
We end the day, forgetting care!

Chiseled Moments in a White Wonderland

In the frosty air, I slip and slide,
My snowman's nose is a veggie side!
With lopsided eyes, he gives a grin,
As I snowball fight with my own kin.

With hats awry and scarves askew,
We waddle like penguins, who knew?
Snowflakes twirl, a dance in flight,
Our cheeks are red, a comical sight!

I built a fort, a snowy domain,
But my brother's siege caused me great pain!
Snowballs fly like ninja stars,
We laugh so hard, I drop my bars!

In this white world, we play and play,
Mischief lurking at the end of the day.
Winter's joy, a giggly scene,
Chiseled moments, funny and keen!

Frost-Kissed Fables of the Future

A snow-covered hill, my trusty ride,
On a sled that's barely fit for a glide!
But off I go, like lightning fast,
Screaming 'wee' till I hit the grass!

Snow angels made, with arms wide out,
Angelic forms, or so we shout!
But I roll in, my halo's askew,
Instead of grace, I fall like a shoe!

An epic snowball, I think I threw,
But it missed the target, what a view!
My friend is soaked, all giggles and glee,
Next round she vows it's revenge on me!

Frosty tales wrapped in laughter's glow,
Each winter's day, we steal the show.
In this winter's fun, we carve our fate,
Frost-kissed fables, never too late!

Shadows Cast by Snowy Reveries

Footprints in snow, a clumsy ballet,
I tripped over nothing, oh what a display!
My shadow leaps on a snowy scene,
As I tumble down, in winter's machine!

A snowball pact with friends in tow,
But who will strike first, I do not know!
With laughter loud, our cheeks aglow,
In this winter war, it's all for show!

Hot cocoa spills from my frosty mug,
A sip on my lip, I'm feeling snug!
But wait, what's this? A frosty plume,
As I laugh it off, I meet my doom!

As shadows stretch in the fading light,
We chase our dreams with snowball delight.
Winter whispers, "Make memories,"
In shadows cast, we dance with ease!

Dreams Unfolding in the Frost

With snowflakes falling, a dream takes flight,
We twirl and spin in the pale moonlight.
Warmed by laughter, cheeks all aglow,
Underneath starlit skies, with a playful flow.

A carrot stick for a frosty lip,
My snowman looks ready for a road trip!
With mismatched mittens and floppy hats,
We giggle at our snow-covered spats.

The snow is deep, the day is bright,
A snowball toss, what a thrilling sight!
But as I throw, I falter and slip,
Landing face-first, oh what a trip!

In frosty dreams, we build and play,
Creating joy on this winter day.
With every laugh, the chill blows away,
In dreams unfolding, we find our way!

Painted Footprints in Fresh Snow

With every step, a dance we make,
In winter's blanket, a giant cake.
My boots are artists, bold and bright,
Leaving prints that spark pure delight.

Snowball fights, the laughter flies,
As frosty flakes fall from the skies.
My friend slips down, a comical sight,
We both burst out laughing, pure delight.

The world is quiet, hushed and white,
Yet humor blooms, a snowball fight.
Each frosty breath, a puff of glee,
In a winter wonderland, just you and me.

Hats askew and scarves like tails,
Chasing each other, leaving trails.
In this winter play, we're full of cheer,
Let's make some memories year after year.

Impressions of Winter's Quiet Majesty

The world is draped in icy lace,
But watch me tumble, a clumsy grace.
I try to glide, but oh, I fall,
My dignity? Gone! Who cares at all?

Snowmen stand like stately kings,
While I decipher what humor brings.
With carrot noses and buttons bright,
They wink at me in the pale moonlight.

Snowflakes whisper, "Time to play!"
As I trip on the ice, what a display!
With every slip, I laugh out loud,
Winter's majesty wrapped in a shroud.

Now is the time for joy and mirth,
As winter shows off her frozen girth.
We share this world of chill and cheer,
In snowy laughter, we persevere.

Frostbound Moments: The Sculptor's Touch

Sculptors of silence, we call the frost,
With snowflakes as dreams, not a moment lost.
In snowy fields, we leap and twirl,
Who knew winter could make us swirl?

The sculptor inside me wants to play,
To mold and shape the white ballet.
But oops! Down I go with a splat,
Snow on my nose—how about that?

Frosty fingers and rosy cheeks,
Unplanned portraits, giggles, and squeaks.
We build our castles, or at least we try,
With laughter echoing high in the sky.

In this frozen art, I find my home,
Amongst snowflakes where wild imaginations roam.
Each slip and slide, a masterpiece made,
In frosty moments that never fade.

A Symphony of Snowflakes: Stillness Composed

A quiet tune in the snowy night,
Each flake a note, perfectly right.
I dance with my shadows, oh what a show,
Tripping and spinning in a snowflake glow.

Neighbors peep through frosted glass,
As I pirouette, too proud to pass.
The snow whispers secrets, cold and true,
But all I hear is 'Laugh, it's for you!'

Every snowfall, a new refrain,
With giggles and chuckles mingling in the rain.
Ah, winter wonder, pure and bright,
Turning my fumbles into pure delight.

So pause a moment, hear the sound,
Of winter's symphony all around.
In the stillness, find the fun,
A frosty adventure has just begun!

Whispers of Frost-Covered Dreams

In a world of chilly cheer,
Snowflakes dance, oh so near.
They tickle noses, icy bright,
While kids giggle with sheer delight.

Mittens lost, and boots that squeak,
Creating snowmen, cheek to cheek.
Carrots for noses, they proudly flaunt,
While snowballs form in a lively jaunt.

A slippery slide, oh what a thrill,
Who knew winter could be such a spill?
Falling down, like clumsy pros,
Rolling laughter, where no one knows.

So grab your sled, let's speed away,
Through powdery paths where we all play.
With frosty whispers and giggles bright,
Let's cherish this chill, with pure delight.

Sculpting Silence Beneath the Chill

Snowflakes gather, soft and white,
On rooftops high, what a sight!
Squirrels leap, a snowy race,
All crammed in a cozy space.

With each flake, a story told,
Of winter's charm, and days so bold.
Snow angels prance, arms flung wide,
While snowmen smile, full of pride.

A cup of cocoa, oh so warm,
While whispers swirl, a chilly charm.
Furry hats, and tongues out there,
Catch each flake floating in air.

Let's sculpt the laughter, freeze the glee,
Winter's canvas, wild and free.
In this frosty, whimsical hold,
We find the joy that never grows old.

Etched in White: A Winter's Lament

Blanket of snow, oh where to tread?
Each step a giggle, strike with dread.
Feet slip and slide, a funny show,
Chasing the dog, who thinks it's a go.

Frosty whiskers on all the trees,
Tickling branches in the breeze.
Fallen branches, a tangled mess,
Watch your step, oh what a stress!

Snowball fights that spark old dreams,
Flying fluff and silly screams.
With snowflakes landing on our chins,
The best of losses, laughter wins.

So here we stand, in winter's grasp,
Finding joy in cold's clasp.
An eternal jest, so soft and clear,
In winter's joke, we find our cheer.

The Last Dance of Icy Feathers

Whirling snowflakes take to flight,
In a pirouette, oh what a sight!
They spin around with frosty grace,
In a chilly waltz, at a brisk pace.

Frosty cheeks and laughter loud,
In winter's feast, we feel so proud.
Sledding down the hill so steep,
With giggles echoing, joy we keep.

Falling softly, a light embrace,
Catching snowballs at a rapid pace.
A flurry of giggles in the cold air,
As frozen whispers float everywhere.

So let us dance in snow's delight,
Through fields of frost, till fade of light.
In this swing of winter's cheer,
We frost our hearts and spread the year.

Crystals in the Frosty Air

Tiny flakes dance down with glee,
A snowflake boogie, wild and free.
One lands on my nose, a chilly tease,
I sneeze and laugh, oh what a breeze!

Snowballs fly, a playful fight,
I duck and roll, what a sight!
Laughter echoes on frozen ground,
In this winter's joy, pure fun is found.

A snowman's hat? A pointy cone!
Oh no, it's a carrot! Looks like a loan.
His face grins wide, melting away,
I guess he won't last until May!

Snowflakes whisper, secrets shared,
Each flurry a giggle, winter's caring.
Underneath the sky so bright,
Frosty fun, a pure delight!

Breath of the Chilling Future

Chilled air bites, but spirits soar,
We sip hot cocoa, still wanting more,
With every laugh, the frost does fade,
Winter's joke, a slippery trade!

Snowmen waddle, a clumsy crew,
One loses a nose, oh what a view!
He stumbles and fumbles, arms go wide,
In this frosty dance, there's nothing to hide.

Sleds zoom by, a race to win,
But who will crash? Let the fun begin!
With giggles and squeals, we crash and slide,
In this winter wonderland, we take pride.

Breezy whispers, snowflakes spin,
Gales of laughter crammed within.
Tomorrow's chill holds nothing wild,
Just playful fun for every child!

Impressions on the Canvas of Cold

Brush the ground with purest white,
The canvas awaits, a snowy sight.
With boots like brushes, we stomp around,
Creating art on frozen ground.

A snow angel flops, but oops! No wing,
Just a blob that makes us sing.
With giant paws, we draw and play,
Winter's gallery in full display!

Snowflakes twirl, a painter's dream,
Colors of white, the world does gleam.
With giggles loud, we march in line,
Creating chaos, a masterpiece fine!

Frosty fingers wave goodbye,
As snowflakes tumble from the sky.
Tomorrow's canvas is set to show,
More silly fun in the winter's snow!

Sketching Shadows on Shimmering White

On a canvas of shimmer, we make our mark,
Our shadows dance, igniting sparks.
With twirls and jumps, each scene comes alive,
In this wintry playground, we thrive!

Chilly giggles beneath the sun's glow,
Creating memories in the soft snow.
A splash of laughter, a dash of cheer,
The shadows remind us of fun's frontier!

Snowball chuckles in the frosty light,
A friendly duel, winter's delight.
Bounce and roll, let the cold win,
In this snowy play, we find our grin!

Frigid whispers swirl all around,
Painted laughter in the snow so profound.
Tomorrow awaits the icy cue,
With silly strokes, we'll start anew!

Enchanted by the Frosted Flight

With snowflakes flying, there's much to do,
A snowman's hat becomes my shoe!
The carrots are lost, and the scarf's gone wide,
A penguin looks on, slightly mystified.

With laughter in the air and snow in my hair,
I twirl in the whiteness without a care.
Each slip and fall leads to endless cheer,
It's a winter wonderland full of good beer!

The sledding slope beckons with joy untold,
But I launch like a missile, a sight to behold.
A tumble and roll, then I pop up with glee,
"It's just winter yoga!" I laugh, "Look at me!"

Snowball fights rage, I take my best aim,
Then turn and get clobbered—oh, who's to blame?
With snow on my face and a grin ear to ear,
I wave to my foes—"Shall we have more beer?"

Mysterious Sculptures of a Snowy Path

The snowdrifts whisper tales at night,
Of shapes and forms that give a fright.
I saw a snow fox wearing a hat,
And a snowman dancing, imagine that!

As I stroll along, the shadows leer,
Are those footprints? Or just my fear?
A rabbit with style hops in delight,
Wearing sunglasses, what a sight!

The trees stand tall, dressed up in white,
Like they're all off to a winter fight.
A squirrel is plotting—what's next to steal?
Those acorns look good, it's a great big meal!

Snowflakes catch laughter as they swirl,
The frost will hold tight, let's give it a twirl.
With a laugh in the air and starlight above,
The snowy path sings of all we love!

The Artistry of Winter's Embrace

In this chilly world of white and blue,
I sculpt a snow angel, just for you.
But somehow I land with my nose in the frost,
Now my halo's a donut! What a funny cost!

I fashion a snowball, ready for battle,
But my dog steals it—I hear him rattle!
He launches it back, a fetch with a twist,
In this ballet of snow, I can't resist!

A frosty ballet, each step a new joke,
With snowflakes waltzing as my poor back broke.
But who needs grace when you've got such flair?
As I slip and slide, like I just don't care!

The art of winter brings giggles and cheer,
With each frosty masterpiece drawing us near.
A snowman's bowtie, askew on his chest,
In this gallery of fun, I feel truly blessed!

Frosted Footprints of Possibility

With every crunch beneath my feet,
I leave behind laughter, oh so sweet.
Each print a story, a tale to unfold,
Of sleds and snowballs, and winter's bold!

A mighty snow fort, strong as a rock,
But it wobbles and shakes, oh what a shock!
My friends take their aim, but wait—what's the plan?
A snowball target? I'm a brave, brave man!

With mittens all floppy and noses aglow,
I dance like a penguin, stealing the show.
The trees all chuckle, I swear that they do,
When I trip on the ice—oh what a view!

Frosted footprints mark this day of delight,
A tale in the snow, bold and bright.
With giggles and glee as we all make our way,
These whimsical paths lead to fun and play!

The Sculptor of a Frosty Future

A chisel made of snowballs, oh what a sight,
Whittling illusions, with sheer delight.
Every flake a giggle, every carve a cheer,
We sculpt our giggles, while sipping chilled beer.

With frosty mittens and hats askew,
We're laughing at penguins, who don't have a clue.
The ice is our canvas, our playground of glee,
Shaping snowmen with dreams, as wild as can be.

A snowman with shades and a funky bow tie,
Strutting down the lane, oh my, oh my!
His carrot nose wiggles, he's quite the charmer,
Dancing in winter, the ultimate farmer.

So grab a good buddy, let's sculpt till we drop,
We'll roll frosty boulders and never will stop!
Laughing and tumbling, we'll make quite the scene,
The sculptor of winter, jazzy and keen!

Tomorrow's Chill Captured in Crystal

Snowflakes fall lightly, like whispers of joy,
Each one a secret, no need to deploy.
Tomorrow's chill glimmers like diamonds so bright,
We'll capture it laughing, till late in the night.

A snowangel flops, making shapes in the white,
An abominable giggler, what a silly sight!
With each frosty tumble, we're losing our cool,
As snowflakes conspire, we're playing the fool.

Snowball fights erupt, with giggles and squeals,
Dodging frosty missiles like summer's hot meals.
Tomorrow's chill hides beneath layers of fun,
Take that, wise winter—our day's just begun!

So here's to the frost, and the joy that it brings,
To laughter and snow, and sprightly out-sings.
In this crystal wonderland, carefree we'll roam,
Tomorrow's chill captured, we've made it our home!

Frost Etchings on the Edge of Time

Frost etchings appear like doodles in the air,
Sketching icy giggles, with whimsical flair.
On windows they pop, a dance of delight,
Spelling out secrets that frolic at night.

We're drawing snow swirls, with laughter so bold,
Tickling the cheeks of the young and the old.
Let's make frosty critters, with mischief in tow,
Painted in snow, as the warm breezes blow.

Each flurry a story, each chill an embrace,
Whispering mischief, with giggles we chase.
The frost's like a canvas, let's etch it with cheer,
Turning moments to magic, with each passing year.

So come join the fun, in this frosty, bright land,
Time's slipping away, let's give it a hand!
With frosted laughter and frosty old rhyme,
We're etching the magic, on the edge of time!

Whispers of Ice and Velvet Skies

Whispers of ice dance upon velvet skies,
Tickling our senses with frosty goodbyes.
A giggle erupts when the snowflakes collide,
Each twinkle and tease leads us out for a ride.

With sleds like tiny rockets, we fly down the hill,
Squeals of delight, what a glorious thrill!
The night's painted silver, as we twirl and we spin,
In this winter's embrace, let the fun times begin.

Frost-covered laughter makes snow-capped dreams,
We're sculpting our futures, or so it seems.
In this frosty wonder, we're masters, you see,
Creating our ruckus, it's pure revelry!

So raise your hot cocoa, let's toast to the night,
Underneath snowy blankets, where the stars shine bright.
With whispers of ice, and our hearts set a-fly,
We'll keep on the fun till the morning draws nigh!

Silence Woven in White

In a world wrapped tight in a cold embrace,
Snowflakes giggle, they float with grace.
Hats go flying, scarves dance away,
Oh, what a circus beneath the gray!

Pants soaked through, kids tumble and roll,
Snowmen are lopsided—what a sight to behold!
They sport a carrot, and buttons quite wide,
Nature's own jest, with pride they abide.

A cat leaps out, its whiskers all frosted,
Looking for warmth, it feels quite exhausted.
Twirling like fairies, the flakes are a treat,
Each step we take is a wintertime feat.

Silence so loud, it tickles the ear,
Chasing our laughter, the joy is quite clear.
The world is a canvas, so vast, so grand,
And all of us here, just kids in the sand.

Frosty Musings on a Blank Canvas

There's a canvas out there, all fluffy and white,
Where angels took flight in sheer delight.
We plop down our bodies, make snow angels sing,
The giggles erupt, oh what joy they bring!

Each flake that falls whispers secrets untold,
Of battles with snowballs, and snow forts bold.
One slip on the ice, and whoosh! Down we go,
Like plump little penguins on winter's wide show.

Hot cocoa awaits, with marshmallows piled,
While laughter and chaos make winter so wild.
"Let's build a giant!" I shout in delight,
But the head turns out flat, oh what a sight!

So we bake little cookies, all frosted and bright,
With a sprinkle of joy, they vanish in the night.
The kitchen's a mess, but who really cares?
Just a bunch of snowflakes in cozy warm chairs.

The Chiseled Dreams of a Bitter Wind

The wind howls with laughter, a mischievous tune,
It nudges the snowflakes like dancers in June.
They tumble and spin, in a frosty ballet,
With noses all red, we shout hip-hip-hooray!

The ground's a white wonder, a slippery slide,
We race down the hill, no caution, just pride.
But one rogue snowblock lies waiting for me,
I'm airborne for seconds, and land like a tree!

Puffed cheeks and whispers, the magic is real,
We tuck in the snowmen with smiles like a meal.
Carrots for noses, but what's with the hats?
One's dressed as a pirate — where are your gnats?

Around us the laughter is loud and sincere,
As winter wraps us in its chilly veneer.
With skies painted gray, our giggles collide,
In this frosty world, we let humor reside.

Frosted Whispers of Tomorrow

In a blanket of white, we giggle and play,
Tomorrow brings more, who knows, come what may?
With snowball fights brewing, a sneak attack here,
We launch, we duck, with shouts of good cheer!

The sun peeks through, oh, what a sight,
Melting the edges of our snowy delight.
But wait, is that chocolate, I smell from the shop?
Time for a treat, who's ready to hop?

With cheeks all aglow, we embrace the chill,
Stepping through snowdrifts, we wander at will.
The world becomes magic, a sweet winter's dream,
With laughter and stories—a warm, silly theme!

So let's raise a toast, to the flakes in the air,
For every soft drift, let's all stop and stare.
With snowmen and giggles, our frosty delight,
We'll cherish this moment, in laughter, unite!

Milton Keynes UK
Ingram Content Group UK Ltd.
UKHW022116251124
451529UK00012B/549

9 789916 941874